Inspired
by
Angels

SINDA JORDAN began receiving messages from the Archangels Michael, Raphael, Gabriel, and Uriel in 1993. Over the course of a year, the angels dictated many different inspiring lessons, which Sinda compiled into letters for everyone to read.

Each angel can provide loving guidance for specific problems in everyday life and can be called upon accordingly:

Michael, with his benevolence and compassion for all of humanity, can be called upon when we are in need of loving assistance.

Raphael, the physician of the angelic realm, can be asked for assistance when we are faced with any type of healing challenge.

Gabriel, with his talent to aid us in dissolving fear, prepares us for change and gently guides us through it.

Uriel, with his watchful eye, helps us see our path more clearly; he can be called upon when we need his clarity to help guide us.

"Discover the comfort and joy that these angelic messengers bring to your life. Allow their love to enfold you and guide you through the still, gentle voice in your heart."

Inspired by Angels

Letters from the Archangels Michael, Raphael, Gabriel, & Uriel

Sinda Jordan

Blue Dolphin Publishing
1995

Copyright © 1995 Sinda Jordan

Published by Blue Dolphin Publishing, Inc.
P.O. Box 8, Nevada City, CA 95959
Orders: 1-800-643-0765
http://www.bluedolphinpublishing.com

First hardcover edition: May 1995
First softcover edition: August 1998
ISBN: 1-57733-044-7

Library of Congress Cataloging-in-Publication Data

Jordan, Sinda, 1954–
    Inspired by angels : letters from the archangels Michael,
 Raphael, Gabriel, & Uriel / Sinda Jordan.
        p.   cm.
     ISBN 1-57733-044-7
     1. Spiritual life.   2. Angels—Miscellanea.
 3. Spirit writings.   I. Title.
 BL624.J657   1995
 291.2'15—dc20   95-5876
                                                       CIP

Cover design: Lito Castro

Printed in the United States of America
 10   9   8   7   6   5   4   3   2   1

Dedication

I WISH TO DEDICATE THIS BOOK to the four Archangels who brought forth their messages through me, and to all the human angels who appeared at just the right moment to lend a helping hand or an encouraging word. Your loving acts of kindness have touched my heart, and I am grateful for your assistance.

Table of Contents

Introduction

MY FIRST REAL UNDERSTANDING of the Archangels began with an article I read in 1993* It was an interview with author/psychologist, Dr. Joan Borysenko, regarding her beliefs on the presence of Angels, especially the Archangels. In the article, Dr. Borysenko described how she invoked the four Archangels to be present with her every day. At various times throughout my life I had heard the names Michael, Raphael, Gabriel, and Uriel, but I never knew who they were—I didn't even know they were Archangels! I had been meditating for years; however, I was so inspired reading about this respected psychologist and her belief in the Angels, that I began to ask for their presence when I meditated.

I found that just asking for the presence of these Angels made a significant difference in my meditations. When I specifically asked for their presence, I always felt a warm, loving feeling. But one day, while just relaxing, I suddenly began to feel in my heart a warm,

*New Age Journal, May/June 1993: "Mind, Body, Beyond" by Peggy Taylor.

loving feeling, and I hadn't even asked for the presence of the Angels, nor had I been thinking about them. And then a thought came through my mind which I knew was not my own. "If you write, Michael will come," he said. I did not know what to make of this message at first, but the next day I sat down and began to write the messages that were coming into my mind, knowing that they were not my own thoughts—that they were somehow "inspired."

The "letters" in this book were dictated through me over the course of one year, from July 1993 through June 1994, from Michael, Raphael, Gabriel, and Uriel. They have been inspirational to me in my spiritual growth and physical healing, and now I feel these messages will help others.

The first to communicate was Michael. Michael has a benevolence and compassion for all of humanity. His love for us knows no bounds. He is the peaceful warrior who speaks to our hearts and compels us to take action. He carries a mighty sword made of pure love that cuts through all that is false. Michael's presence may be called upon whenever you are in need of loving assistance.

The second Archangel to make his presence known to me was Raphael. He has many gifts and talents but is best known as the physician of the angelic realm. Raphael understands the nature of dis-ease in our minds and bodies, and through his compassion he gives us his gifts to aid in our healing. Ask for his assistance when faced with any type of healing challenge.

Gabriel was the next Angel to bring forth a message of hope. One of Gabriel's talents is to aid us in dissolving our fears so that we may truly feel the love within our hearts. This Archangel is devoted to humanity and is often present during times of change. Gabriel prepares us for change and gently guides us through this process.

Finally came the wonderful messages of discernment from Uriel. This Archangel has many special gifts, one of which is the ability to help us see our path more clearly. Uriel's watchful eye is a sincere blessing. It is to your greatest advantage to call upon Uriel's gifts of clarity to help guide you.

It is possible for every individual to form a personal relationship with the Archangels and receive their loving guidance. Their desire to love and serve humanity is immense. Discover the joy that these angelic messengers bring to your life. Allow their love to enfold you and guide you through the still, gentle voice in your heart.

Although these writings touch on many different subjects, they bring a universal message of love. Listening to your inner knowing is one subject that is repeated many times. The Angels would be the first to encourage you to take their messages within and discern what is true for you.

I am sharing these writings with you to support and encourage you. My hope is that you will develop a personal relationship with the angelic beings who watch over you, guide you, and unconditionally love you.

When you develop an awareness of their presence and invite their participation into your life, magical things begin to happen. I feel we have reached a time in our history when, more than ever, we need to believe in miracles. We need to restore our hope and rebuild our faith. When we honor the presence of Angels in our lives, hope and faith abound.

Acknowledging the Angels has allowed me to soar and give my heart wings. I give thanks every day for the joy and love Angels have brought into my life. From the beginning they were present, helping me and assisting me, even though I did not readily acknowledge them.

I hope these letters will help you become more aware of the essence of Angels and their love for you. Listen to the gentle stirrings of your intuition, and know that the Angels are communicating with you. Open your mind, and allow the loving guidance of the Angels into your heart. They are the messengers of God, and they rejoice in your joy.

Inspired
by
Angels

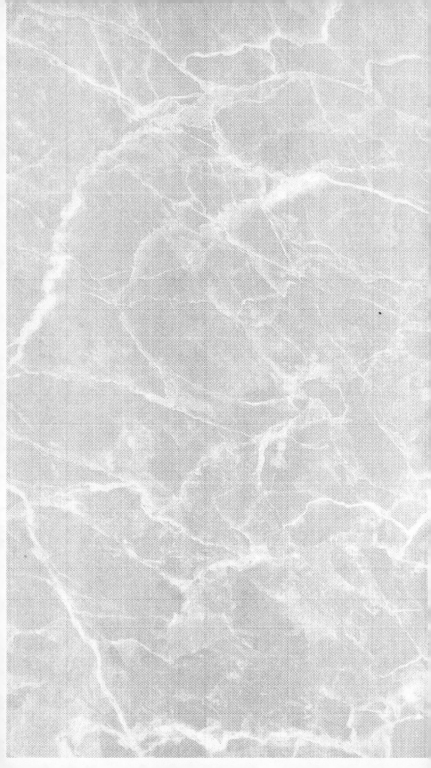

Be Aware of
Your Thoughts

⌢ Michael ⌢

GOD IS NOT A PUNISHING GOD. You need only to receive divine love through your heart to feel the full power of God's love. It is your thoughts of fear, anger, and hatred that keep you from feeling God's love in your heart and lifting you to your true state of awareness. You attract to you that which you send forth in thought.

We, who watch over you and bring loving guidance, must transcend great layers of denseness created by your thoughts. When you discipline your thoughts, the denseness around you is lighter.

Be aware of the creative power of your thoughts. Use this power to repair and rebuild yourself in God's light.

Become an example of peace and harmony in your own life. Start by looking in the mirror and healing what is reflected back to you. Then, and only then, can you serve as an example of God's love working through you.

Can you truly say your house is in order? When the thoughts are disciplined, right action follows. The way to achieve disciplined thought is through meditation. The stilling of the mind allows the mind and the heart to connect as one.

The Search Is Within

⁐ Michael ⁐

LIFE IS MADE UP OF MANY CHALLENGES. God's love, light, truth, and wisdom will guide you through these challenges to proper action. It is important to ask for God's counsel to meet these challenges with guided light.

Be silent and still. Feel God's presence in your heart. Feel God's love radiate through you like a warm sun. Be still, and in the silence, you will know the truth.

You are seeking; you are searching. The search is within yourself, that is where your answers lie. They are buried deep within you, waiting to be awakened in the silence. All you need to know is already inside you waiting to be received.

Develop a Joyous Attitude

☞ Raphael ☜

BE JOYOUS IN YOUR THOUGHTS, ACTIONS AND DEEDS. The feeling of joy brings you closer to God.

Joyousness is an aspect of love that is lacking on the planet. The joy that exists in the present moment, the joy that you feel inside and express to others, is God working through you.

When you are joyous, certain chemical impulses occur in your body. These impulses are capable of healing the body of blockages that impede the flow of energy. When you can express the feeling of joy, despite your external circumstances, healing takes place.

Joy and love are very closely related. As you incorporate and express these feelings in your life, you will heal your separateness from God.

Strive to be joyous in your work, in your play, and in your relationships. Celebrate life with a joyous attitude, and the light of God will surely shine through you. This is how you light the way for others. Be still and feel the joy of life fill your heart and your body.

Dissolve Fear with Love

⌐ *Gabriel* ⌐

WHERE THERE IS FEAR, THERE IS THE ABSENCE OF LOVE. Love and fear are never present in the same place. The releasing of fear requires trust in a higher power with a loving purpose. This divine guidance is accessed through your heart by stilling the mind.

When you enter the silence of meditation and receive God within your heart, you will dissolve your fears with the power of love.

Fear is a very crippling emotion and leaves great devastation in your body. In the stillness, feel the fear leave your body as it is replaced by love. Feel the lines of worry vanish from your face and the weight lift from your shoulders. Feel the tightness in your stomach dissipate as you become free from fear.

Release your fear and receive God's love in its place.

Profound
Decision-Making

⌒ Uriel ⌒

BE SURE-FOOTED. This means knowing when and where to place your feet. The key to being sure-footed is discernment. More than a doer, you are a decider. In order to be a decider, internal knowing must take place. This leads to mental clarity.

Through meditation the chatter in the mind becomes stilled, and you receive God's counsel. The quieting of mental chatter leads to clarity and profound decision-making. There are no wrong decisions, only lessons to be experienced with varying outcomes. Most of these lessons may be learned with minimal discomfort. There is always a way through any given situation when God's counsel is sought.

It is not in your best interest to make your decisions in an emotional way. You believe that when you consult your heart, you are consulting your emotions. This could not be further from the truth. When you consult the heart, you receive God's love and guidance. The inner voice of the heart will quiet the emotions and keep you cool and calm in the face of great stress.

The way to access God's love and guidance is through prayer and meditation. Believe in the divine guidance within your heart. Then put forth your question to God in the form of a prayer, and expect an answer. Still the mind and enter the silence to receive God's counsel from within your heart. The final step is to give thanks for the guidance you have received.

This is how you communicate with God. This is how you respond with love in any situation. Allow your heart to guide you with God's love and wisdom.

Recognize the Divine in Others

⌒ Michael ⌒

IT IS DIFFICULT FOR YOU TO UNDERSTAND SPIRITUAL LOVE when you do not yet understand physical love. Physical love is only one aspect of a loving relationship, but too often it becomes the main focus for expressing love between two people.

This physical love, or romantic love, brings vitality and passion into the relationship and serves to strengthen the union. The union is formed to balance some aspect of the personality that needs healing. A balancing takes place between the male and female aspects of your nature.

When romantic love is misused, however, it creates separation and confusion, which promotes dis-ease. The misuse of romantic love has contributed to substantial ill will throughout the planet. When spiritual love is sought and is the focus of a relationship, the ill will becomes transmuted into goodwill or God will.

What is spiritual love? It is the recognition of the Divine in another person. When you find spiritual love in your relationships, you become humbled to the Divine in every aspect of your life.

Divine love spurs you on. It opens gateways of creativity and the desire to give without concern for receiving. Receive you must, however, because spiritual love opens your heart to higher levels of loving. Your heart gently opens and God's love penetrates your heart.

Spiritual love asks for no less than an unconditional desire to serve love and to give it away to uplift and fulfill the healing needed in another.

Embrace the Present Moment

⌒ *Michael* ⌒

ENTER THE SILENCE TO QUIET YOUR THOUGHTS and calm your emotions. In meditation receive the love and light of God and create inner peace within your being. A sense of calm will prevail when you are no longer guided by negative impulses as you have been in the past. There will be a quickening in your heart and mind, which gives you a renewed sense of purpose.

Releasing the past is necessary in order to embrace the present moment. In this way your present moments are fresh and new and not built on old, limiting patterns. The release process need not be painful, only complete. Your pain is the body's way of reminding you of your past and thereby holding you to limiting patterns that are familiar.

Be gentle with your body. It will benefit you to include it in the release process. Cooperation between the body, heart, and mind is the key to total and complete release of old, limiting patterns of behavior. Thank

12

the mind and body for showing you the limitations to which you still cling.

During meditation bring your mind and body into alignment with your heart for guidance. Ask to release the past and all its limitations to the love and light of God. Allow the light of God to radiate through your heart and dissolve the negative thoughts and emotions that currently emanate from you. Fill your being with inner peace.

Heal While You Sleep

☞ Raphael ☜

ASK THE ANGELS TO COME BE WITH YOU AT NIGHT while you sleep. There is much that can be done to aid in the healing of your physical body. Please allow us to help you.

Healing of the body requires love and light to be guided within the body to the blockages that obstruct the flow of energy. The love and light of God may be called forth by all who need it.

However, it must be asked for, and it must be received. In order to receive this healing energy, the conscious mind must first allow it. That is why this type of healing is best accomplished while you are sleeping. The conscious mind is less likely to interfere during this time.

Why would the conscious mind keep you from receiving? First, because it does not believe that healing can be attained in this way. Second, because above all else it wants to be right. So, by disallowing the healing

14

energy to flow freely into the body, the conscious mind gets to prove that this type of healing does not work.

Self-sabotage happens often when the conscious mind clings to limiting belief systems. This does not mean that you should try to sever the conscious mind from the healing process. It needs the love and light of God as much as any other aspect of your being. But when the conscious mind is allowed too much power over the whole being, then imbalances occur within the body. The body must create a great deal of drama to get your attention.

Let the conscious mind know how much you love and care for it, but that you need it to let go of limiting beliefs that no longer serve your growth. Ask it to allow for the common goal of inner peace and perfect balance among body, heart, mind and soul. When this is done, there is no limit to the healing that may be experienced.

Be an Example
of Self-Love

☞ Michael ☜

WHEN YOU NURTURE YOURSELF WITH LOVE, you set an example for others that loving the self is vital and necessary. When you put all of your loving energy into fulfilling the needs of others, you rob them of the opportunity to fulfill their own needs and discover self-love. It is dangerous to teach others that they must always seek love from outside themselves, as it sets them up for feelings of guilt and failure.

Seek the kingdom of heaven, which is love, from within. Nurture that feeling, and allow it to grow and flourish through all of your being. To create dependency through love stagnates all growth. To create self-reliance through love generates growth and higher awareness. Remove guilt and control from the loving process. Your goal is to be an example of self-love and to reflect that loving self to others.

The love you wish for others will always be there when you love yourself first.

Make Friends with Your Pain

☞ Raphael ☜

IT IS TIME TO RELEASE THE PAIN. In order to do this you must first love the pain, for it can teach you.

To love the pain is to recognize how it serves you, without giving it the power to control you.

Pain stops you in your tracks and makes you take notice of your body. It is a blessing when used in this way. It gets your attention and allows you to reassess the situation.

Go into the silence, and ask your body what it needs to tell you. Thank it for calling attention to this aspect of your being that was limiting your growth. Then ask your body what is needed at this time to create balance and harmony once again from within.

Bring your body into alignment with the heart, the mind, and the soul, and it will serve you well. Try to separate your body from the process, and it will become very dramatic in order to gain your attention.

Your body needs to be loved and nurtured as much as the mind, the heart, and the soul. All must work together to create inner peace.

Talk to your pain. Give it love and understanding the same way you would comfort an injured child. Make friends with your pain and it will no longer be your enemy.

You have the power to heal when you use the power of love. Locate the separation within your body and send it your love. This will work like magic.

Knowledge Comes from the Heart

☞ Uriel ☜

KNOW THAT YOUR CHOICES ARE GUIDED BY LIGHT. Take action based on the knowing that comes from the heart. The heart is the center for all knowledge—all knowing takes place in this center first. Listen to your heart and you will find that there is wisdom in your choices after all.

There are no mistakes, only different avenues of learning. Some avenues are easier than others. When you ask to know God's will in your heart, these avenues for learning are illuminated for you to see more clearly. The pathway is first lit through the heart and then understood by the mind.

Enter the silence and truly know your own heart, where the path of light and love will unfold for you to see more clearly. Once you allow yourself the joy of being in your heart, the doing will be effortless. There will be no need for endless worry over your choices. Proper action will shine before you. You will find that

19

less energy will be required for the accomplishment of your goals when the heart is consulted first.

Know that God's will is made known to you by entering the silence and allowing your heart to guide you. There is always a way through any situation when you allow God's will to guide you.

Communicating with God through your heart is the first step in any decision. The mind will delight in this new source of counsel. It will gladly give up the confusion generated by the counsel of conflicting outside sources.

Listen to the loving voice within your heart, and you will no longer fear the decisions in life. Trust your heart to bring God's counsel into every decision you make from this day forward.

Receive Divine Guidance

⇌ Uriel ⇋

STILL THE MIND AND ENTER THE SILENCE; then listen to God speak to you through your heart. Allow the heart to counsel the mind. Feel the joy of being guided by light.

You are never alone in times of decision. God is always ready to guide you, but you must ask to know God's will and receive this guidance within your heart. God's will may be sought, but it is never forced. Imagine a life where your decisions are filled with light and love. This life is yours for the asking. All who seek God's counsel will receive it. You must learn how to receive that which is sought after. Your heart is the key to receiving God's will. With the light and love of God as your counsel, how can you doubt your choices? When you pray, you are asking for God's counsel. When you enter the silence and still the mind, you are receiving God's will through your heart. You will feel the truth of God's wisdom and be guided with divine light and love. All that is needed is for you to ask for God's counsel and trust in the inner knowing from your heart.

Develop a Loving Attitude

☞ *Michael* ☜

LOVING THE SELF IS A CONCEPT that few truly comprehend. It is honoring the spark of God that resides inside of you. Be loving and nurturing to the self, create sacred space around you, and take the time to develop your inner gifts and talents. These are all ways of loving the self and should not be confused with being selfish. In order to live in balance and harmony, it is necessary to love the self as much as you love others.

Allow yourself to be nurtured without criticism. The mental chatter of judgment and criticism is extremely self-defeating. It sends a message of unworthiness to all of your being.

Be thankful for the opportunities given for self-love and nurturing. Develop an attitude that says time spent nurturing yourself is time well spent.

When you love the self, you are loving God, because God lives as an ever-present spark of light inside you. Nurture the self and you increase the light radiating from you. Allow your light to shine through the joy and happiness of self-love.

Be very generous in the time spent nurturing your mind, heart, body, and soul. Show to all of your being the same love and respect given to others and you will experience true joy and happiness.

Create Unity Within

Raphael

WHAT IS PAIN? Your pain is a symptom of your struggle. Stop struggling and start allowing. When you fight against your pain, it becomes the focus of your attention. You give it power to control you.

Ask your body to remember what it would feel like without the pain. Have your body take you back to a time when there was no pain. Ask to have your body reconstruct the feeling of being without pain in the present moment.

Do this daily so that your body can practice having the feeling of being without pain. Your body is capable of healing any aspect of itself in this manner.

Your conscious mind wants to have control over your body rather than work with it in loving partnership. This is why the body and mind need direction from the Higher Self, through the heart, to create harmony, peace, and balance.

Without loving guidance from the Higher Self, there will be a constant struggle between the mind and the body to gain total control.

When the Higher Self is the guiding force, the mind and body work together to benefit the total being.

Pray to have your body, heart, mind, and soul always in total cooperation with each other. Then enter the silence and allow these aspects of yourself to work together in complete harmony.

Increase Your
Powers of Observation

⌒ Uriel ⌒

BECOMING AWARE OF YOUR THOUGHTS is the first step in learning how to discipline them. Notice the thoughts that you have throughout the day. Learn to observe your thoughts without judgment.

Meditation is an excellent way to increase your powers of observation. When you enter the silence, many hidden thoughts surface and become conscious.

Allow your deepest thoughts to surface and observe them with love. This will reduce their power over you. When a thought appears and you try to hide it, you give it power. It is impossible to hide any part of yourself from God. The inner struggle produces feelings of depression and unworthiness. God loves all of you unconditionally. If a thought appears that is negative, allow it, observe it, then release it. There is nothing in you that needs to be hidden. Allow the stillness of meditation to illuminate and release that which is buried deep inside of you. This will help you discipline your thoughts and think in a positive way.

Release the Need to Worry

◦ Gabriel ◦

RELEASE THE FUTURE TO GOD and allow it to unfold at His will. By overcontrolling life's experiences, you lose sight of the opportunities available to you in the present moment. When you release the past and the future to God, you relinquish control to a higher power.

Your task is not to worry over what has been or what will be, but to focus on the joy and happiness that exists right now. All power takes place in the present moment. Be loving and joyous now. Do not postpone your happiness to some future date. There is evidence of God's love and light all around you at all times.

Look at the world through your heart, and you will perceive a different world than the one you have been viewing. Allow your fears to surface and release them one by one. Watch their power over you dissolve, and see joy and love take root in their place. There is much to be thankful for in every moment. Let this be your focus, and the future will take care of itself. It is in very capable hands.

27

Meditation Brings Clarity

⟨ Uriel ⟩

THERE IS MUCH LOVE that goes into presenting opportunities for your growth. The challenge lies in using your free will to make choices for yourself.

It is to your greatest advantage to ask to have your will guided by God's will. The uniting of God's will with your own makes your free-will choices work for your highest good.

The stillness of meditation allows you to unite your will with God's will. Meditation brings clarity to the mental process by allowing the heart to be involved in all your decisions. It is through the heart that God speaks to you.

Too often the mental chatter of your thoughts keeps you from knowing the counsel of your heart. When you enter the silence and quiet the mind, you receive inner knowing from deep within your heart. In the silence, God's will shall be known to you. The practice of meditation opens the doorway to more joyful and rewarding experiences in life.

28

Stilling the mind removes the confusion and chaos of unguided decisions. When practiced daily, meditation connects you with your inner knowing and enables you to choose the path of least resistance. Set aside a specific time each day to meditate, and make this appointment with God your first priority. Your mind will become more receptive if you meditate at the same time each day.

The way to develop inner knowing is through dedication to the practice of receiving it through meditation. Make your choices with complete confidence by stilling the mind and listening to the loving guidance from your heart.

Discern Truth
Through Your Body

⌁ Michael ⌁

LET US SPEAK OF TRUTH. Truth is God like love is God. Truth is a gift given to you to make your life brighter. It brings light to all who hold it. It is difficult to find examples of truth on the planet today. That is why it is so important for each of you to light the way by living a life of individual truth.

There is much confusion over what truth is. Truth stands alone. It speaks for itself. It asks for nothing other than to serve. It is never self-righteous. Its properties are very similar to love. Like love, truth is found in the heart.

Ask your heart to show you what truth feels like. Become acquainted with this feeling. Make friends with it. Practice experiencing the feeling of truth so that you are able to recognize this feeling in any situation. When you enter the silence to meditate, ask to know the truth from within your heart.

As you go about your day, notice how your body reacts to what you hear and say. See how many times you can recognize the feeling of truth within your body when you are exposed to a thought or an experience. Read a book. Listen to your friends. Observe how your body reacts to what you see and hear. Begin to discern when you have experienced truth and when you have not.

Your body can be a great asset to you in the discernment of truth. Notice what happens in your body when you are not receiving the truth. Notice what happens in your body when you do not speak the truth. Much can be learned through exploring what truth feels like.

Through prayer and meditation, ask God to enlighten you about truth. Once this has been mastered, it will be very difficult for you to be deceived.

Search for Truth Within

☞ *Uriel* ☜

THE TRUTH THAT YOU LONG FOR IS AN INNER TRUTH. It is an inner knowing and understanding. Searching for truth from outside yourself can bring pain and heartache. It is possible to receive truth in the words that you read and from the counsel of others. What is lacking is your ability to discern the truth from these and other sources. The only true source for knowing truth is within your own heart.

The search for truth must first take place from within the depths of your being. What is missing is your ability to receive and know your inner truth. Make the search for inner truth a personal quest. It is one of life's greatest adventures.

Explore your inner being through the stillness of meditation and know yourself; know the truth from within your heart. This process will clear much of the confusion that now exists in your body and mind. When you can reach down to the core of your being and know what truth feels like, you will be able to discern with ease the truth from any source.

You know the truth from inside of yourself already, but you have separated yourself from this knowledge. You have separated yourself from God. It is time to heal the separation and know and understand the truth once again.

Your body and mind will come alive with the sensation of truth. You will be remembering what already exists inside of you, and the separation will heal. Pray to know that which you already know, then go into the silence and receive God's truth.

Truth Dissolves Fear

☞ Gabriel ☜

LEARN TO USE TRUTH TO ENHANCE YOUR LIFE. Be grateful for the recognition of truth as you go through your day. Begin to observe how many times throughout the day you choose to ignore the truth. Do not judge yourself for these acts, but begin to observe how you are feeling in these moments. What are the circumstances that make you choose to ignore truth?

There is much that can be learned when the self is observed with love instead of with critical judgment. Begin to observe how you allow external circumstances to pull the self from the path of truth. These self-defeating patterns of behavior can be transmuted and released through prayer and meditation.

Allow the self to know and understand the power of truth. Know that the truth is the way through any given situation. Make the search for inner truth through meditation a priority in your daily life. Speaking truth, living truth, and being truth will bring a new kind of freedom into your life. You will no longer live in fear, because truth and love dissolve fear.

Be diligent in your pursuit of truth from inside yourself. Learn to communicate truth at all times. Truth is the way of God. Truth will set you free.

Access Your Guides

⌒ Michael ⌒

BE GRATEFUL FOR THE TIMES SPENT IN SILENCE. That is where all knowledge and understanding take place. You strengthen your connection with God when you meditate. You learn how to access your guides in the silence.

You have many teachers who wish to help and guide you on your path. Their assistance can enhance your life greatly. You need only to ask for their assistance through your heart, and knowing will take place.

Enter the silence and receive this guided knowing. Help is always there for the asking. The key is to ask and then to receive.

Prayer and meditation bring forth the teachings of the ancestors. Always give a prayer of thanks for the information received. The Universe likes to hear gratitude. It is the sign of a humble heart.

Be Aware of
Your Motives

⌒ Michael ⌒

THERE ARE TIMES WHEN THE TRUTH needs to be expressed in as few words as possible. At these times it is important to be aware of the person or persons doing the listening. It is possible to be overwhelmed by more truth than one can comprehend. It is important to consider those who are receiving your message. When truth is used in this way, it does not become a tool for feeding the ego.

The question to ask yourself is, "Who is being served by the need to give forth this information?" Is the ego looking for admiration or is there a sincere desire to uplift another? The key is whether or not your counsel was sought. Truth can cause pain and harm to another when it is given purely to satisfy one's ego.

Only volunteer what you know when you are asked specifically to do so. Then respond with truth to the best of your understanding. It is important not to anticipate another's response or questions. Stay present in the moment and give people your full attention. Learn to listen with all of your heart, and you will learn to speak in the same way.

Nurture Your Inner Truth

⌒ Uriel ⌒

ONE OF THE MOST VALUABLE LESSONS you can learn is when to share your truth and when to hold it. The ability to discern between these two options lies in the counsel of your heart.

Holding truth inside of you for a gestation time is like planting a seed and nurturing its growth. The truth that you hold will expand inside and allow you to grow and develop along with it. As like attracts like, the truth that you nurture within will attract more truth to you.

A time will come when the truth that has expanded within you will ask to be shared. Meditate on the best pathway for it to serve its purpose. Ask to unite your will with God's will so that you may receive guidance for sharing with others. It is important not to force your will but to seek God's counsel.

Learn to discipline yourself to be silent. There is so much more that can be learned in the silence than in the noise of the world. Let the truth spread through you like a beam of light and feel its warmth. The time to share this warmth will come. Be patient and focus on the joys that silence brings.

Let your desire for communication be served by communing with God in your heart first, then with your fellow man.

Never Fear the Truth

☞ Gabriel ☜

AS LOVE AND FEAR ARE NEVER PRESENT IN THE SAME PLACE, the same is true of truth and fear. Learn to love the truth and never fear it. Be diligent in the living of God's laws, and the truth shall always follow. Holding truth inside of you for nurturing and expansion is an act of love, not fear.

The truth does not bring harsh experiences into your life. It is the energy created by your thoughts of fearing truth that generates these experiences. Fear is a crippling emotion that stagnates your growth. Its only positive attribute seems to be its ability to bring you to your knees to seek God's counsel.

The truth need never be feared, but it does require a maturing time within before it is shared. Practice and develop your skills at recognizing truth in every situation you encounter. The fear of allowing new experiences into your life will dissolve when you use the pursuit of truth as the focus.

41

In order to become adept in the discernment of truth, you must first allow openings for new experiences to enter your life. Do not fear life's experiences. They are gateways for understanding your relationship with God. Be grateful for the opportunities that are presented for your growth. Enter the silence and allow the truth from within your heart to dissolve your fears.

Truth Is Different for Each Individual

⌒ Uriel ⌒

THERE ARE INFINITE PATHWAYS TO GOD and all of them need to be honored. It is important to allow other people their own pathways and rites of passage.

Truth is different for all individuals based on where they are on their path. It is possible to share truth for the purpose of guiding and uplifting one another. This type of counsel can be of great benefit when one is feeling stuck or depressed. You must seek out and ask for counsel of this nature. It is possible to cause anxiety in another, when truth is given without thought for the person receiving it.

Pushing someone along their path is a violation of Universal Law. The free will must be honored at all times. To share truth with the intent of controlling another, will bring undesirable results. If you are in doubt as to your true motive, it is better to be silent.

Encouraging others to use meditation for discovering their own truth, honors the free will of the individual. It empowers the person you wish to help through his own capabilities. Teaching others how to connect to their inner truth will bring greater results than making them dependent on you for the truth.

Learn to hold your knowledge and use your understanding to direct individuals to find their own inner truth. Empower those who seek your counsel to know their truth through entering the silence.

Be an Example
of Truth

~ Michael ~

GOD IS ALWAYS LOOKING FOR WAYS TO EXPRESS truth. You are capable of receiving truth in your heart and becoming an individual expression of it in your daily life.

To know the truth, still the mind and enter the silence. To be an expression of truth, live what is in your heart. When you live your truth, you light the way for others.

Be grateful for the examples of truth that you receive throughout your day. Notice the joy that fills your heart when you live your life as an expression of your inner truth.

There is a lot that can be done as an individual to heal the consciousness of the planet. Everyone has the ability to express truth. When you speak the truth from within your heart, others respond with truth. It shows others the way.

Know the truth through meditation; feel it grow inside of you like a well-nurtured seed. Express yourself through truth and be a living example to all you meet.

45

This is how to heal one another. By healing one another, you heal the planet.

Each one of you has an important role. You need to know the truth from within your heart and live it. Be an instrument for truth through personal expression and set an example for others to do the same. Give thanks for the opportunity to serve the planet and your fellow man by living your inner truth.

Honor All Expressions of Truth

⌒ Michael ⌒

TO LIVE YOUR TRUTH IS THE REAL RESPONSIBILITY. Too often you choose to take responsibility for another person's life and pathway. This violates their free will. True responsibility comes in honoring all pathways and being an example of truth.

Notice the times when you choose to become responsible for another. Observe how you are feeling in that moment. What signals does your body give you? Become observant and know yourself. This will help you to know the truth.

In order to honor the path of another, it is necessary for you to honor the unfolding of your own path. When you can truly honor your own path, you will light the way for others. Knowing the self is the first step.

The key to knowing the self is observation with unconditional love. It is in the observation of the self without judgment that the self feels free to unfold and be known. Know that when you observe yourself without judgment you are nurturing yourself with unconditional love.

Prayer and meditation are wonderful ways for knowing the self and observing the self without judgment. Pray for guidance from God through your heart. Meditate and receive inner knowing. Feel the joy of loving the self unconditionally.

Know the truth from deep within and live it to the best of your understanding. Be an example of truth in your daily life. True responsibility is the ability to honor all expressions of God's truth as it is brought forth by each individual.

Responsibility Is
the Ability to Respond

⮑ Uriel ⮐

UNDERSTAND THAT THE ABILITY TO RESPOND propels you on your path. There are many circumstances, many experiences, that make up your life. The ability to respond to these experiences by uniting your will with God's will lights the way. It shows you the way through. When the path is lit, it is easier to discern. When the path is in darkness, you stumble and fall. Uniting your will with God's will is the way to light the path. Ask in prayer for the way through any circumstance, any situation, and then still your mind and listen with your heart to know the way through.

When you react emotionally to outside experiences, the path of proper action becomes unclear. Without clarity you take responsibility for things that are not your responsibility. When you are truly being responsible, you have the ability to respond with proper action. The ability to respond does not include taking responsibility for the learning experiences that belong to others. Learn to allow others to grow through their mistakes and trust that this will further them on their path.

When you take responsibility for the lessons of another, there is an emotional response of resentment and anger, even if it is not expressed. Observe yourself. Observe what need is being served when you choose to take responsibility for another. Observe how your body is feeling. Ask yourself why this feels familiar. Recognize your need to control the path of another by becoming responsible for it. Stop sending the message that others are incapable of proper response. Observe yourself and others objectively, and release the need to take responsibility for the lessons of others.

Create Balance
from Within

⌒ *Raphael* ⌒

THE BALANCING OF UNIVERSAL ENERGY and earth energy within the self will enable you to express yourself with less effort.

Creating balance from within begins by locating your center—the point from which your energy flows. This is the area surrounding the solar plexus. Use your hands to touch this area of your body in order to bring the two energies together consciously and in harmony.

Feel yourself stabilize as you focus attention through your breathing on your solar plexus and balance the energy inside of you.

It may be necessary for you to focus your breathing, while placing your hands on your solar plexus, several times throughout the day in order to maintain a feeling of centeredness.

The energy needed to perform your tasks will be reduced if you are centered first. Focusing the energy on your solar plexus with your breath and hands brings balance to all forms of your expression. When energy is balanced within you, the actions that you send forth require less effort, less energy.

Experience your day with your energy balanced and flowing from your center. Notice the change in the amount of energy required to accomplish your goals.

In the silence of meditation, balance the universal energy and the earth energy that flow within you. Use your breathing and the gentle touch of your hands to become centered.

Release the Illusions
of Separation

⌒ Michael ⌒

BALANCE, HARMONY, AND INNER PEACE are what unify you with God. Harmony is achieved through an alignment of the body, heart, mind, and soul. This alignment allows you to feel connected to God from within. It enables you to express inner peace when faced with external conflict.

Unity allows you to receive guidance from your Higher Self through your heart. To walk in harmony is to walk with God. When the body, heart, mind, and soul are in alignment, greater understanding is available to you from your Higher Self.

Pray to have this alignment take place. Then meditate and observe any blockages to the unity. Remember to observe yourself with unconditional love and without judgment. Release the illusions of separation and create the reality of unity with God from within.

In the stillness, receive your Higher Self, and know the joy of being united with God in your heart.

Open the Flow of Energy

⌒ *Raphael* ⌒

BALANCING THE ENERGY WITHIN YOUR BODY will promote healing.

The removal of blockages within the body is what allows energy to move freely through you. These energy blockages create illness in your body. They are formed by the internalizing of false beliefs and limiting thought patterns.

Meditation and prayer allow you to identify and illuminate the false beliefs that are creating blockages within you.

Pray to know what blocks the flow of energy from moving freely through you. Then, in meditation, receive this knowledge and gently allow the area with the blockage to reveal the false beliefs held there.

It is important to do this process without judgment. To criticize your thoughts gives them power. To observe them with unconditional love dissolves them and opens the natural flow of energy within your body.

Create Sacred Space Around You

☞ Michael ☜

THE LIGHT AND THE LOVE OF GOD IS TRUE PROTECTION. When this is brought forth, you are protected. The protection that is longed for is the protection from invasion into your sacred space. The ability to create sacred space around you and stand centered within your boundaries is an act of self-love.

Use the light and love of God that is within you and all around you to help you set and maintain proper boundaries. Visualize yourself in the center of a circle. See all that you wish to have in your life inside the circle with you. Now visualize all the experiences that you wish to invite into your life, and welcome these inside of your circle. See the light—strong and bright—holding the boundary, keeping your circle sacred. This is true protection—protection through love.

The light of God is love. Loving the self is what creates and maintains proper boundaries. Give thanks for the joy and the peace of mind that is created when you are centered in your sacred space. Give thanks daily for the light and love of God and the joy of being alive. Know the joy of creating and maintaining sacred space around you through loving the self.

In meditation, visualize yourself standing safe and strong within the boundaries of your circle. Do this daily until you no longer need to think about your boundaries—they just are.

The Power
of Forgiveness

⇒ Michael ⇐

BELIEVE THAT YOU DESERVE TO BE JOYOUS, happy, and filled with light, and release the need for punishment. Your desire to be filled with love is strong. Be generous in the forgiveness of the self. This will open the doorway for the forgiveness of others. The power of forgiveness is strong within you; allow it to flow freely through your heart.

To forgive yourself is to experience the true power of love working within you. Your mistakes may be numerous, but you have learned many valuable lessons. Trust that you will never repeat these same mistakes again, but please allow yourself the freedom to make new mistakes and learn new lessons. All has value.

Look at these lessons as opportunities to learn to forgive and allow God's love to flow through your heart. Repeat the words "forgiveness" and "love," and feel the power of these words. You are always forgiven to the extent that you can forgive.

There is love being sent to you every moment of every day. Still your mind and be gentle with yourself in the quiet. Feel the power of love and heal the need for judgment of the self. Live your life with a forgiving heart.

Release the Need
for Limitations

~ Uriel ~

FREEDOM IS YOURS IN WHATEVER EXPERIENCE or circumstance you find yourself. The freedom to be who you are is the freedom you seek. The only limitations on freedom are imposed by the self. By your belief in lack and limitation, you create limiting situations.

Use meditation to explore the need for limitation in your life. It is important to strengthen, not question, your right to be. From this inner strength will come a renewed sense of purpose. When you feel your purpose grow from within, a joyfulness fills your being. A true sense of purpose will dissipate feelings of depression and stagnation.

Pray to know and understand your true purpose. Allow yourself to be all that you were created to be. Release the need to limit who you are. Feel the freedom that comes when you acknowledge the joy of your being.

You Are Forgiven
As You Forgive

⌐ Gabriel ⌐

IT IS TIME FOR YOU TO RELEASE THE FEAR GENERATED by thoughts of unworthiness. The most damaging thought is the fear of not being lovable. It is the deep feeling that your past mistakes somehow make you unworthy of love. This is a false belief. Clinging to it brings pain into your life.

You are forgiven for the mistakes that you have made as you forgive yourself. It is not necessary to know the details of all your past transgressions. It is not necessary to itemize all of your mistakes. It is time to trust in the lessons you have learned and move forward with a joyous heart that lives in the present moment.

Release your doubt and fear, and accept the self-love that forgiveness brings. Be generous with the love that you give to yourself, and generosity will flow from you to others. Pray to open your heart and release the fear.

Death Is Not
an Ending

⌒ *Michael* ⌒

DEATH IS NOTHING TO FEAR. It is life that most people fear. To live your life fully, to be joyous and full of light is the challenge.

If people would learn how to live with joy in their hearts, there would be no reason for them to fear death. Death is not an ending but a continuation of life at a different vibrational level than what is seen on the physical plane.

This altered state is at first experienced as a period of rest and can vary in length of time depending on a person's preparation for the transition. If the transition took place due to a traumatic event, there can be a very long period of rest.

The most important thing that loved ones can do for someone that has departed is pray. These prayers send energy to help the soul in transition.

During the first three days, the magnetic pull of the physical plane is the strongest for those souls undergoing the transition from one dimension to another. Your prayers help light the way and make the transition a smooth one. Group prayer focused on one individual is even more powerful. This is why services of this nature are of great benefit to the soul in transition.

Death is not an ending but an extension of life in an altered state of being.

Develop Your Positive Thoughts and Feelings

⌒ Michael ⌒

YOU ARE MADE OF LIGHT, and you return to this state of being when transition takes place. The physical body is left behind, and you become a body of light.

You are brought gently into this awareness by other familiar beings of light. Your thoughts and feelings are easily read by others when you are in this altered state. You will soon find yourself in surroundings that reflect these thoughts and feelings in a manner similar to that of a mirror reflecting an image.

It is to your advantage to learn to discipline your thoughts and feelings while on the physical plane. Not only will your physical life be more pleasant, but you will greatly enhance your experiences after transition.

Disciplining your thoughts and feelings is different from suppressing your thoughts and feelings. Meditation is an extremely effective way to allow your true thoughts and feelings to surface. You can then focus on your positive thoughts and release the negative, limiting ones.

63

The time to develop positive thoughts and feelings is now, in the present moment. It is a misconception to believe that you will develop this ability automatically after transition. You have a wonderful opportunity in the present moment to alter your current physical experiences and your experiences at the time of transition.

Become aware of your thoughts and feelings. Live your life consciously and be free of fear. Be joyous in the understanding of all that you are.

Heal Your Body
with Love

⌒ Raphael ⌒

THE PHYSICAL SELF NEEDS TO HEAL. Begin by listening to the needs of your body with an open heart and a loving mind.

A harmonious environment must be created within your body in order for a peaceful environment to be created on the planet.

Concentrate on each part of your body, and send it the feeling of being nurtured and loved. This will help generate peace and harmony within your physical self.

Every aspect of your body is important and plays an integral part in the functioning of the whole being. To generate healing, all aspects of your physical self must work harmoniously together.

Learning to love every aspect of yourself, every cell, every atom, will generate healing within the body. When all aspects of your being are nourished with love, peace and harmony are created within.

If there is any part of you that is not receiving love, it begins to feel unworthy. This feeling of unworthiness will generate discord and rebellion within. It will demand your attention and will refuse to be ignored.

The cells of your body need to be disciplined with love. They need to feel worthy of contributing to the whole, and they will do so in perfect harmony.

Enter the silence and allow the cells to receive loving guidance from the Higher Self. Be firm but loving in your desire for perfect harmony from within the cells.

Love your body by acknowledging the contribution that each cell makes to the functioning of the whole being. This will bring about the needed cooperation at the cellular level for healing within your body.

Trust Your Feelings

⌒ Michael ⌒

KNOWING HOW TO LOVE YOURSELF and be loving to others can be confusing at times. A healthy balance between the compassion you show yourself and that which you give to others is essential in order to create a state of balance within your being.

The only sure way to stay balanced in this area is to trust your feelings without question. When you are doing that which feels good to yourself and harms none, you are loving the self. Others may feel they are being harmed because you are not doing as much for them as before. In truth, an example is being set for them to love themselves more effectively.

When you trust your feelings and act accordingly, you give others permission to trust their inner feelings. This is an act of love. To do for others that which they can easily do for themselves is control, not love. Trust your feelings and listen to your heart. Let your heart guide you to a deeper level of loving the self. Then you will truly be able to love others with joy and compassion.

Love Yourself Unconditionally

⌐ *Michael* ⌐

THERE IS SO MUCH MORE TO LOVE than that which is being currently practiced on the planet. It is impossible to have the feeling of loving others if you don't have the feeling of loving the self.

Close your eyes and surround yourself with the feeling of being loved unconditionally by the self. What surfaces, instead of a loving feeling from the heart, is critical and judgmental chatter from the mind. The mind begins to list all the reasons why you are not worthy of unconditional love.

You then turn to others, longing and searching for someone to prove the critical mind wrong. Because of the law of attraction, you can only attract what is in your thoughts. You therefore attract someone who pretends to love you, when in truth they are looking for the same validation of their worthiness to be loved as you are.

To attract true love into your life you must first think loving thoughts about yourself. You must see yourself as worthy of your own love. When your thoughts become disciplined and loving toward the self, you will begin to attract others into your life who are truly loving.

Begin by going within and receive the feeling from the heart of loving the self.

Face Your Fears

≈ Gabriel ≈

LIGHT THE WAY FOR OTHERS BY RELEASING YOUR FEARS. Recognize your fears and make them conscious. Observe them objectively and you gain power over them. Hiding from your fears only gives them power over you, while true courage is the ability to face your fears.

Doing battle with the fear you hold inside increases your inner strength. If more people would do battle with the fears that flourish inside them, there would be an abundance of peace and harmony in the outside world. Learning to confront the negative thoughts and feelings that you harbor inside builds character and strength. And as you conquer your fears, so shall you advance in life.

Give thanks for the opportunities that life provides for the surfacing of your fears. To run away from what you fear gives it great power over you. Go beyond the emotion of the fear to the true feelings that lie buried beneath. Enter the silence to clarify and illuminate the feelings beneath the fear. In the stillness, the mind will release that which it fears. Each time this is done, you advance yourself further on your path.

Spiritual Growth Is Never Forced

⌒ Michael ⌒

THE SPEED AT WHICH YOU PROGRESS ON YOUR PATH is directly proportional to your ability to trust and not doubt the presence of God within you.

Speed itself is a limitation. The perfect speed for spiritual growth is no speed at all, but the acceptance of God within your heart. You must trust that you are already where you need to be and that all is in perfect order.

Open your heart to the joy of your being, and relax in the presence of God's love. Let go of the need for perfectionism, and love yourself unconditionally—with total acceptance. Spiritual growth is never forced but is gently allowed.

Ease up on the pressure you put on yourself to accelerate your growth. Trust in the presence of God within your heart, and receive divine guidance in the stillness of meditation. Simply be the joy within your heart, and trust that the growth you seek will occur effortlessly.

Trust Your Inner Voice

⌒ Uriel ⌒

THROUGH YOUR WORDS IT IS POSSIBLE to help light the way for others. Words of encouragement, hopefulness, and thankfulness are ways to uplift and strengthen others.

Always speak the truth with a sincere and open heart. Beware of statements containing comparisons, judgments, and criticisms. These statements can create fear and anxiety in others.

When striving to help another, go beyond that which is obvious and look to the soul. Encourage others to connect to and rely on their own truth rather than rely on you for the truth.

Trust your inner voice when helping others, and the right words will come.

Break Through
the Illusions

⇌ Uriel ⇋

LACK AND LIMITATION ARE SERIOUS THOUGHT PATTERNS that need to be addressed. It is easy to look around you and see validation of lack in the world. This is but an illusion, for the belief in lack is manifested first in your thoughts.

Look within for validation of what is real. When you look within, you feel the joy of abundance radiating through all of your being. This feeling of abundance will dissolve your thoughts of lack and limitation.

Do not neglect your time spent in silence. This well-spent time is what maintains a healthy outlook filled with joy. When you feel the truth from inside yourself, the illusions of the outside world lose their intensity.

All is possible when you seek God from inside your heart. Unite your will with God's will, then be of good will in the outside world. Let your words spread a message of abundance and joy.

Nurture Yourself with Acceptance

⌒ Michael ⌒

BE GENTLE WITH YOUR THOUGHTS ABOUT YOURSELF. The more gentle you are with yourself, the more loving and gentle you will be with others. The freedom you crave is the freedom that comes with the acceptance of the self.

Be loving to yourself in this moment. Love and accept yourself with forgiveness. Nurture yourself with forgiveness. The loving acceptance of the self is the food your body needs. Learn to love the shadow side of yourself—all of you needs your love and acceptance.

Let go of judgment; you are neither good nor bad. You are in motion, growing and expanding. Allow the shadow side of yourself to surface and teach you. Heal it with love and bring it into the light.

You are what you think you are, so think of yourself in a loving and forgiving way. Take these words within and feel their meaning.

Let Your Light Shine

⌒ Michael ⌒

BE GENEROUS WITH THOSE AROUND YOU. Let the joy in your heart radiate from you to others. Allow the light from your smile to shine. Life is glorious when shared with one another in this way.

Open yourself by being like the rose. Let the beauty of your being bring loving joy to those that you meet along the way. Enter the silence and ask to know the lessons of this magnificent flower. The plants and the trees have much to teach you about God's laws.

Observe nature with an open heart, and feel your connection to God strengthen. The plants, the animals, and the stones hold great knowledge about the ways of God. Take their lessons inside and know their true meaning.

There are metaphors all around you for understanding the nature of God. Pray to understand their meanings; then enter the silence and receive the teachings. Meditations done in nature are extremely powerful.

Experience the Power of Silence

⮑ *Raphael* ⮐

THE PHYSICAL BODY IS A PERFECT CONDUCTOR for universal energy. The energy needs a clear pathway so that it may flow freely within your body.

Negative thoughts create blockages that obstruct the natural flow of energy. When you discipline your thoughts through conscious thinking, these obstructions to the flow of energy dissolve.

Observe your thoughts in the silence of meditation. Is your thinking serving your body or obstructing the natural flow of energy? In becoming a conscious observer of the self, there is much to be learned about your patterns of thought.

Silence is the great teacher. Experience the power of silence. Still the mind and enter the sacred space within your heart. Meditation allows for the development of new patterns of thought while releasing the old, limiting ones.

Through the power of silence you can learn how to speak appropriately. Take notice of your language. Your

77

words are thought in action. Use your words to increase the flow of energy available to you by speaking in positive terms. The resulting changes will clear block-ages and promote healing in the body.

Allow Change into Your Life

⌒ *Gabriel* ⌒

FEAR OF CHANGE IS ONE OF THE MAJOR FEARS that you are experiencing at present. This fear is associated with many deep and hidden feelings. Explore the feelings that surface in your body when you hear the word "change."

There is much that your body can teach you about your hidden beliefs. A need for constant change in your life also signifies fear. Strong feelings of need are often signals for deeply buried fears.

Enter the silence and let your Higher Self teach you. Welcome the chance to observe and accept yourself unconditionally. Explore yourself with a loving heart and a silent mind, to open the doors of understanding in regard to your behavior. All has value when used to promote a greater depth of clarity.

Concentrate your thoughts on the positive aspects of change. Allowing change to flow freely through your life opens doorways for new opportunities that might otherwise go unnoticed. Unite your will with God's will, and welcome all of God's blessings into your life.

The joys of life are available to you in the present moment. Open the doorway by allowing change within your life, and experience the joy that new opportunities bring. Release your fears to God, and trust in the guidance from within. The perfect teacher is waiting inside you, ready to guide you through life's changes.

Be Present Now

⌒ Uriel ⌒

DO NOT WORRY ABOUT THINGS that are not yet in form. Learn to keep your energy focused in the present moment. Experience making decisions from your heart in the exact moment they need to be made. Do not use your precious energy in worry over decisions you are not yet ready to make.

Trust that when the time comes you will make a decision easily and effortlessly, with guidance and assurance. Keep your thoughts focused in the present so you will have the energy to do what needs to be done right now. All opportunity takes place in the present moment. Keeping your thoughts focused in the now allows you to discern proper action clearly.

Perform one task at a time, and see it through to completion before you start something new. Keep your attention focused on what you are doing right now, instead of what you think you should be doing or could be doing. Give what you are doing your full attention.

81

This is how you bring joy and happiness into all of your activities.

Focusing your energy in the present will strengthen your feelings of connection to God during meditation. Be in the present moment so you may make guided decisions quickly and easily throughout your day.

Nurture
the Divine Essence Within

⌒ Michael ⌒

BE ALL THAT YOU ARE CAPABLE OF BEING. Feel the joy enter your heart as you acknowledge the God essence that lives within you. Nurture this divine essence through the acceptance of its presence in quiet meditation. Allow it to teach you of the perfection that already exists inside of you.

Connect daily to this teacher within for instruction, and receive the loving guidance that is present within your heart. Know that you have access to God at any moment. Let each day be a celebration of all that you are. Recognize that what exists in you is also present in everything around you.

When you can acknowledge God within yourself, you will automatically perceive divine essence in others. You will feel connected to all of creation and release any feelings of separation.

The world is a wonderful place when perceived through your heart.

Open Your Heart

⌒ Michael ⌒

THE LOVE YOU SEEK IS THE LOVE OF GOD. God is always present inside your heart. Still your mind, and feel the presence of God within you. Feel the abundance of love that flows through you.

There is a never-ending supply of this loving energy. Open your heart and receive God's love. Nurture every part of your being with this powerful love energy. Feel the tingling sensation throughout your body as you accept and give thanks for this energy.

Love yourself the way God loves you—unconditionally. Your body was created to be the perfect expression of God's love. Every cell in your body will be nurtured with divine love when God is acknowledged from within.

Allow your body to be the temple of light and love it was intended to be. Let God radiate from your heart in all directions until every cell has been touched by God's light and love. All of the love in the universe is available to you through your heart, waiting for you to receive it.

Open your heart and experience love as you have never experienced it before. Then share the love you feel by touching the heart of another. Do this through the gentleness of your touch, the light of your smile, and the compassion of your words. There is a multitude of ways to share with others through loving acts of kindness.

Feel the love and pass it on. There is no need for concern for what you will receive from others in return. There is an infinite supply of love from the universe being sent to you at all times. You need only to acknowledge it, receive it, and be thankful for it. Be generous with the love you give to yourself, and generosity will flow from you to others.

Free Your Mind to Discern

☞ *Uriel* ☜

THE OPENING OF THE HEART is the gateway to inner and outer peace. When your heart is open, unlimited knowing and understanding are available to you.

The most valuable possession anyone can own is an open heart. This does not mean that your heart is left unprotected. Discernment is always present and available from the unified communication between the heart and the mind. Discernment is the truest form of protection.

The heart is where inner knowing is received and shared. The heart is where God speaks to you. Stilling the mind allows the heart to open and receive as it was designed to do. Stilling the mind allows you to receive all-knowing through your heart. This is the source of true knowledge. The mind is then free to choose the most effective course of action. The mind may discern more effectively when no longer burdened with the task of gathering all of the knowledge.

Enter the silence and still the mind. Open your heart and receive all the knowing and understanding made available to you. Trust in the wisdom that comes from the heart, and free the mind to choose the most effective path for action.

An understanding heart is the key that opens the door to higher knowledge. Freeing the mind allows you to discern accurately your opportunities and take proper action. Still the mind and know your heart in the silence.

Create Your Spiritual Temple

⌒ Raphael ⌒

YOUR BODY WAS DESIGNED TO BE THE TEMPLE of your spirit. Your body was meant to be a receiver, equipped with exceptional sensory ability to fine-tune the reception.

Disciplining the physical body increases your sensory perception. Utilizing all of your senses to the best of your ability increases personal awareness.

Increasing sensory perception stimulates a wide range of emotions. It is important to still the mind and allow the heart to dispel the confusion generated by the emotions.

Calming the emotions enables you to receive clarity about the deeper, underlying feelings. The feelings are then registered by the mind to promote proper action. With practice you will have instant understanding under any circumstances.

Dispelling the emotions is best accomplished through the discipline of meditation. A few minutes each day spent in meditation will give you mastery over your emotions.

All forms of discipline—physical, mental, and emotional—strengthen your inner connection with God. The key is balance.

To discipline one aspect of the self and ignore the others increases feelings of separation. Strengthening all aspects of the self breaks down the illusion of separation and increases feelings of wholeness.

Create the spiritual temple that you were intended to be by disciplining all aspects of yourself. Dissolve the illusions of separation within you. Enter the silence to still the mind and open the heart; this will discipline the thoughts and the emotions.

Exercise and observe proper nutrition to discipline the physical body. Do this with a joyful heart and feel the glory of your spiritual temple.

Increase Your Light Vision

⌒ Uriel ⌒

LIGHT IS IN YOU AND ALL AROUND YOU AT ALL TIMES. The darkness you feel is an illusion of separation from the light. To fear the darkness strengthens the effect of its presence.

Visualize a tunnel, and see the light filtering in at the end of that tunnel. Watch the light grow and become brighter and brighter. Do this visual exercise each day, and see the light taking over the darkness of the tunnel until the tunnel no longer exists and there is only light. A few minutes each day of being conscious of the light will help you break through the darkness of your tunnel. Its presence and strength weaken as the light becomes stronger.

Tunnel vision is the strong belief in a world that embodies limitation. It is the belief in a limited number of opportunities and pathways. As the tunnel vision gives way to light vision, the belief in limitation is dissolved.

Light vision allows for the acceptance of infinite possibilities and pathways. Compassion for your fellow man becomes second nature as light vision releases the need for comparison. The thoughts and emotions are greatly benefited by this new and lighter approach to life that accepts infinite possibilities.

There will be a beautiful shift in attitude as you welcome life's experiences with joy and love. Give thanks for the blessings of light vision with a grateful heart and a confident mind, knowing that it exists in total perfection waiting for you to receive it.

Allow Yourself to Be Vulnerable

☞ Gabriel ☜

BEING GENTLE AND KIND IN THE FACE OF FEAR is the task at hand. This is how the heart and mind align themselves to work as one. The unconditional compassion that the heart wishes to bestow creates fear in the mind. The mind is bewildered by trying to protect against this kind of vulnerability. Be patient, and allow the heart and the mind to discover their true purpose. This uniting of function cannot be forced. It must be allowed, with true compassion for yourself in the process.

When you can experience compassion for yourself and the vulnerability of compassion for your fellow man, the need for protection will diminish. When you allow yourself the vulnerability of an open heart, you will be humbled by your own humanness. You will then be able to allow yourself to live your life from the sacred place within your heart without having to protect yourself from the vulnerability this creates.

The protection you seek is from your true humanness and your connection to all that is. The ego demands to be separate from others and therefore protected from knowing and being known. In consciously realizing what you are trying to protect yourself from, the process of dissolving the underlying fear begins. As you acknowledge the similarities with those you meet, the differences disappear and the illusion of separation is dissolved. A true sense of unity fills your being.

Nurture yourself with patience rather than judgment, and allow the process to unfold. Your need for protection will give way to an open heart and the willingness to experience people with love and compassion.

Joy Is a Powerful Force

⟶ Raphael ⟵

THERE IS AN ABUNDANCE OF HEALING taking place in your body. Be joyous and light at heart, and your physical healing will be accelerated.

The energy generated by the feeling of joy is a powerful healing force. Being joyous allows you to see the beauty that is present within you and all around you. It strengthens your connection with God.

The feeling of joy is enhanced when you use humor and laughter to meet life's challenges. Learn to love joyously. Use humor to diffuse heavy emotions. Allow laughter to open the closed doors of your heart. Be joyous in the living of your life, knowing that being joyful is expressing God in action.

Life is meant to be enjoyed, shared, and experienced with love in your heart. Enter the silence to expose those parts of yourself that insist on worry rather than joy. Without judgment, allow the confused thoughts and feelings to surface that keep you from experiencing the true joy of your being. Life was never intended to be experienced through worry and fear.

Allow joy and love to fill the empty places inside. Fill every cell within you with the joy of being alive. Your body will radiate a healthy glow. Your heart will open and shine its light as it was originally intended to do. Your mind will be bright and clear, sending loving thoughts to blaze the trail ahead.

Love Is an Energy

⟜ Michael ⟞

LIGHT AND LOVE ARE THE SAME THING. They both awaken you to the joy of your being. To be filled with light is to be filled with love. To be surrounded by light is to be surrounded by love.

Love is more than an emotion; it is an energy. As an energy, love can express itself in a variety of ways. The emotion of love is just one of love's many expressions. The energy of love is what lifts and restores you to your true state of being. It fills you with a sense of divine purpose.

Loving the self unconditionally opens your heart to receive God from within. Learn to experience the outside world from inside your heart. Feel the comfort of this warm, nurturing home that is present within you.

Your heart is the perfect dwelling and the only true security. Through your heart there is divine presence available to you at all times. Open your heart and receive all that the universe has to offer. Release your fears and explore a limitless universe from within your heart.

Allow your light to shine and fill your inner home with light. Clean away the cobwebs and open up the windows of your heart. Through this opening, breathe the light and love of God into every part of your being. Feel this energy flow through you, healing all that it touches. Let the light inside of you shine so brightly that you are blinded by its light. Then see life through the eyes of God, filled with infinite possibilities and glorious hope.

Nurture and Care for Your Body

ᕽ Gabriel ᕽ

FACING YOUR FEARS TAKES STRENGTH AND STAMINA. Challenging fear is much easier to do with a body that feels nurtured. To prepare your body to do battle with your fears, it is necessary to nurture it with food, rest, and exercise. You feel more courageous when your basic needs are being met. A physical body that feels stressed and full of tension is less likely to meet the challenges that fear generates. To force your body to overcome fear from a physically stressed condition will generally sabotage your efforts.

Begin by listening to and meeting the physical needs of your body in a nurturing way. Then conquer your fears one by one with steady self-assurance. Care for your physical body with patience and love. Use the gentleness of prayer and meditation to allow your fears to surface. Bring forth your conquering hero from within to overcome your fears and move forward on your path, with divine guidance from your heart.

All Cycles Are Relevant to Growth

⌒ Michael ⌒

SLOW AND STEADY IS THE KEY TO UNFOLDMENT. Gentle leaps balanced with quiet retreats help your body adjust to the process of spiritual enlightenment. The leaps are measured by new insights and flexible changes in perception of your physical world. The rest periods allow you to integrate your new knowledge with heartfelt understanding. This understanding in turn elevates your physical body by raising its vibration.

When your physical vibration elevates, the door opens to the next level of spiritual growth. The periods of rest are a very important part of the integration process. If these rest periods in the cycle of spiritual unfoldment are ignored, your body will pull your attention in order to get its needs met. Know that all is in perfect order and there is no need to rush the process of enlightenment.

Allow yourself to unfold one step at a time so that your physical body may benefit from the experience.

Know that all cycles are relevant to growth. Honor these cycles within you and receive their teachings. Rest when it is time to rest, and move forward when it is time to move. Meditate daily and receive guidance from God within your heart. Recognize which cycle you are currently in. When you honor your cycles, you honor yourself with gentleness, patience, and love.

Appreciate Your Inner Beauty

⋐ *Michael* ⋑

BE APPRECIATIVE AND THANKFUL FOR THE BEAUTY that exists all around you. When you appreciate all of God's blessings with gratefulness, you strengthen the love within your heart. It begins with an increased feeling of loving the self and blossoms into feelings of love for all of creation. You begin to know and understand your connection with nature.

Observe yourself very closely the next time you are in a beautiful setting. Allow your emotions to lead you to the deeper feelings just below the surface. What are you receiving from the experience? How does your body feel? Observe your thoughts, are they negative or positive? These simple observations can help you appreciate the beauty that is in you and all around you.

By acknowledging the beauty in nature, you will readily perceive the beauty within people. You will feel a stronger connection to the beauty that radiates from within your heart. When you can honor your own inner beauty, you will surely honor it in the people around you. Learn to appreciate nature with a reverent heart, and you will appreciate yourself and others in the same way.

The beauty has always been there. All that has changed is your ability to perceive and appreciate its presence. Spend time in nature and become quiet and still. Allow yourself to receive the loving energy from the earth, with all its natural beauty.

There Are No Coincidences

⌒ Uriel ⌒

LIFE IS FULL OF MANY COINCIDENCES that seem ordinary at the time. Learning to see these coincidences as divine guidance in action helps you to open new doorways of opportunity. As you awaken to all of the guidance that is available to you, the coincidences in life will begin to increase.

As you consciously realize that there are no coincidences, only God energy expressing itself, you will begin to perceive more of the opportunities that are available for your growth. Life is not accidental but well-ordered and precise. It is just your perception of all that is available to you that needs to be awakened.

When you lose flexibility and become entrenched in a rigid view of life's opportunities, your life becomes an expression of limitation. When your view expands and flexibility increases, your life becomes an expression of abundant opportunities. There is always a way through any problem or situation when God's counsel is sought.

When you expand your limited view of life, more creative solutions to your problems will be available.

These opportunities for growth are always being presented to you, but you must perceive them. Allow the universe to unfold before you. Experience the magic that is present in the coincidences that appear in your life every day. See these as opportunities being provided by God for your growth.

Still the mind and observe the series of coincidences that make up your life. The love of God is everywhere, presenting you with opportunities for higher knowledge and understanding.

Nurture Your Creative Talents

⪜ Michael ⪜

BE CREATIVE IN YOUR PURSUIT OF HAPPINESS. Be prepared to expand your view of life. Love and appreciation of the creativity that is present all around you will open new doors for creative expression within your life.

Focus your attention on something that feels truly creative in your present environment. Focus on its originality and uniqueness. Notice how you feel as you admire its beauty. Do you feel more energized and more creative yourself? Once you have learned to appreciate something, you can create an opening for its presence in your life.

To enhance your creative abilities, begin by admiring the beauty and love that your life represents. True admiration will awaken any latent talents lying dormant within you. Honor your creative talents and provide a nurturing environment for them to grow and mature. This will enable you to become all that you are capable of being. It will also allow you to recognize and honor the gifts and talents that are present in others.

105

True admiration from the heart will clear any feelings of jealousy or envy. Appreciation of yourself and others will expand the loving nature within your heart.

Take time each day to notice someone or something that represents the beauty of creative expression. Be joyous in your heart for the God-given talents that allow you to express yourself creatively in the world.

Raise Your Body's Vibration

☞ Raphael ☜

RAISING THE VIBRATION OF YOUR PHYSICAL BODY is what creates heaven on earth. Your spirit self and your physical self working harmoniously together create total inner peace. This peace is then brought forth from within each individual to create peace on earth.

It is necessary to remove the barriers that are within and dissolve all the illusions of separation between your physical self and your Higher Self.

The natural energy that exists in nature from mountains, rivers, and forests will help you raise the vibrations of your physical body. Raising the body's vibration enables it to hold more energy. As your body increases its ability to hold more energy, it increases the heart's capacity to receive and give love.

The gift of energy is given freely from the earth in the form of plants, stones, and places of beauty. When the energy places of the earth are destroyed, the ability to increase personal energy through nature is also destroyed. What you hurt and damage in nature, you hurt and damage in yourself. Use the gifts from plants and stones to teach you of your connection to the earth.

You are less likely to harm that to which you feel connected. Begin by nurturing your personal environment—your body, your home, your yard, your neighborhood. Take time to rest in the energy of streams and forests. Allow your body to recharge itself through nature, to meet the challenges and opportunities of life with abundant energy.

Create heaven on earth within your physical body. Heal the maladies that exist within you from energy depletion. Focus on the beauty that is present all around you, and feel your energy increase.

The earth lovingly gives you the gift of energy through beauty.

Discover the Power of Co-Creation

⌒ *Raphael* ⌒

THE ART OF HEALING IS AVAILABLE TO ALL. Healing the body is the ability to perceive the false beliefs that have been internalized within you. These beliefs create blockages that obstruct the natural flow of energy in the body.

God does not punish or bring maladies to you. Man brings these conditions on himself in order to increase the illusion of separation between man and God. The individual ego wishes to remain separate so that it can create independently of God. When the individual ego understands that all is available through co-creation with God, it will gladly allow the body to be an expression of God's will.

When you understand that God did not create the maladies that exist within you, your body will no longer feel powerless to alter these conditions. You will begin to feel the real power that comes from co-creation with God. You will know that you can alleviate the illusion of separation, generated by your false beliefs, through true unity with God.

The maladies that you create are, in reality, ways of generating self-importance. They are the individual's attempt at creating independently of God. When the creation gets out of hand and ill health is present, you blame God in order to render yourself powerless to change the situation. You oscillate from being an all-powerful creator to a powerless victim in order to balance your creative ability.

The true way to balance your creative ability is to connect with God from within your heart and enter into a power alliance of co-creation. Discipline yourself to receive God's will in the silence of meditation. This will reduce the need for self-importance and replace it with self-acceptance.

See Yourself Clearly in the Reflection of Others

❧ *Gabriel* ❧

FEAR DEPLETES YOUR ENERGY faster than anything else. There are many false beliefs that have fear at their core. All of these cause the body to lose energy and lower its vibration.

Recognizing these false beliefs within yourself can be difficult, but it is possible to identify these patterns clearly in those around you. The patterns of fear that you see most clearly in others are the ones that are present in some degree within yourself.

You increase your energy when you release the false beliefs that generate fear within you. Shedding light on your fears brings them out of hiding. Exposing fears to clear thought dissolves them. Once a fear is dissolved, it no longer has any power over you. You are then free to think differently and generate new, more rewarding experiences in your life.

The releasing of limiting fears propels you forward and increases the energy available to you. Each fear that

111

you expose and release advances personal growth. Look at others with an open heart and be grateful for what they reflect back to you. It is one of the best ways available for seeing yourself more clearly.

Hiding from others helps you hide from yourself. See yourself as clearly as possible through the reflection given by others. Be sure to observe with love and acceptance. Never hide from what you find disagreeable in others. Instead, listen with an open mind and a loving heart to receive the healing insights they offer.

Reflect on what you observe without judgment or criticism; then meditate on the insights that you receive. In the silence you will see yourself more clearly and receive an abundance of understanding and clarity.

Listen with All Your Heart

⁓ Michael ⁓

TO COMMUNICATE TRUTH YOU MUST SPEAK from your heart, with your attention completely focused on the listener. When this is done, observe how easily your words flow and how your energy increases. The exact opposite happens when you try to force the words by focusing attention on yourself. The thought is formed, but the energy required to communicate the thought is lacking because the focus of attention is concentrated on yourself rather than on the recipient of the information. Notice the energy you feel when others focus their full attention on you while you are speaking.

In order for true communication to take place, there must be an exchange of energy that flows between the people involved. When someone is talking to you, give them your full attention. Listen with all of your heart, and focus on the divine essence that is present within the person speaking. This will add energy to their thoughts and empower them with clarity.

When you focus on the divine essence that lives within each individual, you receive clear insight from God through other people. When communication is shared with focused attention, all parties involved are honored, respected, and given energy to bring forth the truth.

Cultivate the Art of Conscious Listening

☞ Uriel ☜

THE ART OF LISTENING IS WELL WORTH CULTIVATING. The first step in conscious listening is to focus all of your attention on the person speaking. This will bring forth the other person's thoughts and ideas with the maximum amount of clarity. The next step is to notice, without judgment, the thoughts that divert your attention from listening. Allow these thoughts and feelings to surface, but do not focus your attention on them. Instead, again focus your attention on the person speaking. With practice, conscious listening will become effortless.

The ideas that surface when you are listening to another will continue to form if you keep your attention focused on conscious listening. Most people fear they will lose their ideas if they don't express them immediately. The opposite is true, if you keep your attention focused on listening. Trust that when it is your turn to speak, you will receive the energy needed to bring forth your ideas with clarity.

When you are given energy through conscious listening, an abundance of truth and wisdom is brought forth from within you. When you are listened to, you feel honored and respected.

Conscious listening will increase the inner knowing available to you during meditation. When you focus your full attention on the divine essence within your heart, a greater depth of understanding is available to you while meditating. Learn to listen with all of your heart, and give others the attention and respect they deserve.

Be of Service to Others

⌒ Michael ⌒

THE LOVE THAT YOU GIVE TO OTHERS through service heals the separation from God within your heart. Loving service needs to be given freely, without feelings of guilt, obligation, or attachment to results. Live from your heart, and use your gifts and talents to serve humanity.

When service is given with an open and loving heart, healing is present. Give thanks for the opportunities to serve your fellow man. Be grateful for the healing that is given and received. Be generous when you are asked to help. Know that when you help another, you strengthen your inner connection with God.

Meditate on the ways that you can be of service to others. Allow any feelings of resentment or anger to surface. Observe these emotions without judgment and allow them to teach you. When you release the emotions created by your false beliefs about service, you become free to use your gifts and talents for the benefit of your fellow man. You will feel a greater sense of purpose from within you.

Experience the joy of service through an open and loving heart, and develop a passion for giving. Know that your soul expands and elevates when you help another soul on its path.

A friendly smile given to another at just the right moment is a form of service. Too often you feel that service can only be provided in some grand way. Look to your heart and know your true motives for giving. Are you using service to create self-importance, or are you giving through service to provide joy for another? By observing your self without judgment or criticism, you will be enlightened as to your true motives. You are seeking truth for the purpose of expansion and growth.

Always observe yourself with love and acceptance. Meditate on the ways you can be of service to others, and do what flows from your heart without resentment or obligation attached. Honor your gifts and talents, and be of service to your fellow man.

Follow the Path
within Your Heart

⌒ Uriel ⌒

YOU WORRY TOO MUCH ABOUT THE CHOICES that are before you. Follow the path that is in your heart. The path may be paved with obstacles, but if you listen to your heart, you will know the way.

Live your life expressing the truth that is in your heart and you will set an example for others to do the same. It is important to encourage others to feel the truth from inside themselves.

There is an infinite number of ways for truth to express itself. Convey to others what you believe the truth to be for you, not what you believe the truth should be for them. This removes the need for conflict and power struggles over who is right. Honor all pathways for the expression of truth.

Allow and encourage others to bring forth the truth from within their hearts. A wealth of understanding becomes available when information is exchanged from the heart. Always remember to discern the value of shared information by incorporating what feels right to you and releasing the rest. This is the way you exercise control over yourself without trying to control another. It releases the need for argument and encourages heart-felt communication.

When you communicate from the heart, you expand your understanding of the truth. Learn to speak the truth from your heart. Learn to listen and discern the truth through your heart. There are opportunities available every day for enhancing your ability to give, receive, and discern the truth.

In the stillness, allow the mind to focus loving energy on the heart. Your heart will bring forth the truth and guide your life with inner knowing and understanding.

Become a Co-Creator

⌢ Michael ⌢

YOUR HEART IS THE CENTER FOR INNER KNOWING and understanding. Your mind is the core for creative thought. Your body is the temple of expression for creative thought and inner knowing. The alignment of your body, heart, and mind creates an inner peace, balance, and harmony essential to co-creating with God.

Observe any thoughts or feelings of separation that presently exist between these aspects of yourself. Enter the silence and align your Higher Self with your body, heart, and mind. Create the feeling of complete unity and dissolve all beliefs of separation. This will bring forth a greater depth of creativity from within you.

God will express joyously through you when your resistance to wholeness has been dissolved.

Wisdom Comes From Inner Knowing

☞ Uriel ☜

TODAY WE SPEAK OF WISDOM. To understand what makes a soul truly wise, you must understand what wisdom really is. Wisdom comes from an inner knowing of God, which cannot be taught but can be brought forth. Wisdom is attained when thinking and feeling are in unison within an individual.

To be wise is to act from your inner knowing. It is an integrity that exceeds common standards of behavior. Wisdom comes to you when you are capable of acting from an internally developed code of ethics that is applied to everyone without regard to personal outcome. It is the ability to act for the highest good of the whole without concern for the individual ego. This does not mean that the self is sacrificed, because you are included in the good of the whole. You will no longer use the manipulation of others to benefit the self. Responding with inner wisdom transcends the need to control and manipulate others in order to receive for the self.

122

Wisdom, truth, and love are God expressing through you. There is an infinite number of ways for wisdom to express itself. It is not a gift limited to a select few but available to all. Everyone has the ability to bring forth wisdom from within themselves and share it with others. Anyone can focus his attention on another for the purpose of bringing forth inner wisdom. When wisdom is shared, understanding is increased for all.

To be wise is to be kind and gentle to yourself and others. The wise man has no need of harshness or arrogance. Through wisdom he has discovered true gentleness and humility. The stillness of meditation provides the environment needed for wisdom to grow and develop within you. The seed of wisdom has already been planted by God within your heart.

Enter the silence to nurture your inner knowing, and you will be provided with wisdom to guide you through any situation. Wisdom is knowing the appropriate action to take at any given moment. Know your inner voice and be loving, joyous, truthful, and wise.

Feed Your Body
Peace of Mind

Raphael

CARE FOR YOUR BODY WITH REVERENCE and give it the respect deserving a temple of God.

Heal your body with loving thoughts. Your body is an accumulation of confused thinking. Clear the confusion and free your body to be a healthy and joyful expression of God.

See your body as deserving of your love, the way God is deserving of your love. A body that is nurtured, loved, and honored carries you forward through life with ease. Your body will not thrive in an atmosphere of neglect and disdain. You believe that your body has betrayed you, but in truth, it is your negative thinking that has betrayed the body.

It is time to release your false beliefs and fill your mind with loving thoughts about your body. Enter the silence and give your body peace of mind to feed its longing. Your body may feel uncomfortable at first because it has become accustomed to the negative chatter that it receives from the mind. The body will soon cherish the silence and release the need for the chastising to which it has become accustomed.

Meditation allows the mind to be still, which in turn exposes negative patterns of thinking. Be patient with your body for it will resist that which is unknown to it even when what is known causes it pain. With gentle persistence, your body will soon welcome the stillness of meditation and be grateful for the release that it brings.

Be creative in helping your body meet the challenges of meditation. Meditate in a way that feels good to your body and it will cooperate more fully with the process. Ask yourself what makes your body feel comfortable, supported, and relaxed. Then use these tools to help make meditation a joyful experience.

Treat your body with the reverence it deserves, and live your life consciously as a temple of God.

Allow Yourself to Love and Be Loved

⪻ Michael ⪼

LOVING OTHERS IS NOT A TRAP. Love will not bind or control you. Sharing love with people brings beauty and joy into your life.

You are waiting with expectation for the pain to come when you love and care for others. Your anticipation of this pain attracts it to you. Your false beliefs are the trap. The experience of obligation and betrayal is formed first in your mind.

Allow yourself to love and care for others, and allow others to love and care for you. There is no bondage created by loving except in your own mind. There is no need to be afraid of loving others. The false beliefs you hold about love are what generate the fear. Observe these beliefs without judgment and allow the true feelings that are buried beneath them to surface.

People bring joy and understanding into your life. You provide the pain, with the false beliefs you hold about love. It is impossible for you to be manipulated by

126

others when you do not think of using them. Generate thoughts of sharing love with others for the purpose of healing. Your desire to share will attract others to you.

The false beliefs that you hold about loving yourself and others creates the fear that keeps the dream of sharing from becoming a reality. Clear from your consciousness the fear that is generated by confused thoughts and feelings. The door will open wide for a life of sharing with others on many levels.

Experience the joy that comes from allowing people into your life. Release your fears and share the light from within your heart with those on your path. Your light will continue to grow brighter when it is shared.

Give Yourself the Gift of Patience

⌐ *Michael* ⌐

WHEN THERE IS CONFUSION IN YOUR DESIRES, you lack the clarity necessary to create beneficial changes in your life. Confused desires will generate confused goals.

The ability to know and understand the wants and needs of your heart is the first step in receiving clarity. Why do you want to initiate this change? How do you believe this will benefit your life?

Concentrating on one desire at a time will also dispel confusion. This will reduce the scattered feelings that surface when you try to concentrate on too many changes at once. A step-by-step process will reduce stress and add clarity to accomplish your goals. This also allows the body time to experience the benefits or anxieties created by one change before more are created.

Give your body time to adjust to the desires of change generated from within your heart. This will reduce stress and anxiety in the body. Change that creates lasting and beneficial effects involves a unified cooperation by all aspects of the self.

128

Give yourself the gift of patience. There is no need to rush the changes in your life. All is in perfect order. You have all the time you need to initiate the changes you desire. Pushing the stream creates stress, while allowing a gentle flow creates effortless movement.

Be still and listen to your heart. What are your heart's desires? In the silence, allow your mind to know and understand the wants and needs of your heart; then allow your body to feel the benefits or anxieties that each desired change creates. The loving counsel from your heart will allow you to create the desired changes that will benefit your growth.

Allow the Heart
Its Gentle Voice

⌒ Michael ⌒

THE ACHING YOU FEEL WITHIN IS YOUR HEART longing for expression. Let your heart know that you are ready to listen. In the silence, the heart may be heard and understood.

Your mind has a great mistrust of your heart. It blames your heart for the difficulties in your life because of the heart's desire to grow through experiencing the unknown. These challenging experiences create your greatest opportunities for growth. Nevertheless, your mind clings to what is known rather than risk experiencing the unknown. Your heart yearns for new experiences and continued growth. When your mind can allow the heart its gentle voice, you will be able to gain unity and inner peace.

Each new opportunity that is presented for your growth creates thoughts of fear and anxiety in your conscious mind. The conscious mind only wants to experience what is familiar to it. The desires of your heart are never felt or explored because they become overshadowed by the negative chatter from your mind. When this process is continually repeated, the patterns of limitation become deeply ingrained.

Meditation will break the cycle of limitation from the negative chatter of the conscious mind by allowing your heart the silence it needs. In this nurturing silence, your heart will be allowed to express its most vulnerable desires. When these desires are acknowledged, openings will be created for new growth experiences.

Listen to your heart and allow it to become your guiding voice. Set your heart free from the walls you have erected that keep it suppressed and silent. Honor your heart by meditating daily, and live free from your patterns of limitation and fear.

Unlock Your Mind

⌒ Uriel ⌒

YOUR UNDERSTANDING OF TRUTH will increase by opening your mind. An open mind allows for greater flexibility and opportunity in life. A mind that is open has released the need for limitation and accepts growth through change. It knows the joys that new experiences bring.

An open mind allows the truth to be expandable and flowing. What is true for you today may not be true for you tomorrow. The truth expands and grows as you expand your limiting beliefs. When you integrate new ideas with heartfelt understanding, you create greater truth to ponder.

Truth has no beginning and no end; it is limitless. No one person has cornered the market on all of the truth. But when individual truth is shared, each person expands on it according to his level of understanding. Take shared information within yourself to feel what is true for you and release the rest. This is the way you discern the truth.

You create limitation and fear when you cling to someone else's truth. If something doesn't feel like truth to you, let it go. There will be other opportunities presented to receive this understanding. In this way you are patient and loving to yourself. There is no need to force the truth; it comes when you are ready. The truth is always present when you are ready to receive it.

In the silence, still your mind and allow it to open to the expanded ideas being presented to you. Some of these ideas are thoughts shared by others. Some are generated by your own inner knowing. All is available to you when your mind is open and flexible.

Unlock your mind and release it from the limiting thoughts to which it clings. Nurture your mind with exposure to new ideas and allow it to thrive.

Life Creates Worthiness

☞ Raphael ☜

YOUR BODY HEALS FROM THE JOY IN YOUR HEART and creates disease from the limitation in your mind. There needs to be joy in your mind as well.

Allow your mind to create joy in your life by releasing the accumulation of limited thinking. The mind will become a master at creating joyful thoughts about yourself and others. The mind needs to believe that you deserve to be joyful, that you are worthy of experiencing joy.

This may sound absurd, but your mind generates an abundance of thoughts centered around unworthiness. The mind has a tendency to believe what it hears. This is especially true of the messages received from the self.

Notice what you say about yourself to others; then notice what you say about yourself to yourself. This can be a very enlightening observation. If you wrote down the number of times you said negative things about yourself, you would be alarmed. If you heard these remarks from others all day long, you would become angry and depressed. But you continue to listen to the chatter from your mind, internalizing every negative thought until your body becomes ill.

The silence of meditation helps break the cycle of negative chatter and allows the mind to receive unconditional love from the heart. When the mental chatter ceases, the beliefs of unworthiness begin to dissolve. The mind accepts the truth that life creates worthiness, so there is no such thing as an unworthy human being.

When these misconceptions are dissolved, you begin to think joyously about yourself and others. The mind will generate joyful thoughts when it releases all beliefs of unworthiness. Forgive the judgments that the mind has imposed on the self, and think your way through life joyously.

Exposing Fear to the Light

⌐ Gabriel ⌐

THE LIGHT OF GOD IS AVAILABLE FOR ALL TO RECEIVE. Light is the universal energy of life. The light within your heart has the power to dissolve your fears. Fear lives in darkness and is unable to survive the radiance of the light.

Your fears feed on ignorance and superstition, and they keep you from knowing the truth within your heart. If your personal truth creates fear within you, you are dealing with false beliefs, not truth. The truth will never generate fear, only more truth, more love, and more light.

The practice of meditation allows you to recognize your fears consciously. Hidden within the darkness of each fear lies the glorious light of truth. In the stillness of meditation, allow your light to shine brightly and dissolve the walls that keep you living in the darkness of fear.

Have courage and bring forth the light to conquer the enemy from within. The only weapon needed to do battle with fear is the power created by stilling the mind in meditation. In the silence, allow the light from your heart to illuminate your entire being—dissolving the darkness that leaves you fearful and weak.

To be strong is to face your fears and become fearless. Your fears control your thoughts and actions when you give them the power of belief. Release the false beliefs of doubt and unworthiness that generate fear within you.

Receive the light of God from within your heart. Give the light the power that you so readily give to your fears and watch them dissolve one by one.

Happiness Comes from Within

⌒ Gabriel ⌒

CURRENTLY YOU BELIEVE THAT YOUR HAPPINESS depends on outside circumstances. This is a false belief that limits your happiness. If your happiness is totally dependent upon outside circumstances, then there can be no happiness.

You do not need to be trapped by your beliefs into waiting for your joy to appear. It is always present within your heart. Allow yourself to be free from experiences for a time in order to establish a deeper trust in the joy of your being.

When you become dependent on constant activity in order to create the feeling of happiness, you become trapped in that pattern. Ultimately, you will create sorrow because the feeling of happiness fades with the completion of the activity. It is then necessary to generate more activities so you can achieve the feeling of being full.

The feeling of being full is associated with contentment and happiness. In order to experience true happiness, the quest for fulfillment must take place within.

Discover the joy and freedom that exists in the emptiness of experiences. Challenge yourself to face the fears that living in the emptiness brings to your mind. When you get past the fears and allow the emptiness to encompass your being, you will find a freedom never before experienced. In the absence of experience, you will find God within your heart.

When you can learn to welcome the emptiness into your life, your fears will dissolve and you will experience a great peace from within. You will finally know the happiness you have longed for, because it has always been present within your heart, totally independent of outside circumstances.

The Journey Is More Important Than the Goal

⪜ Michael ⪝

REMEMBER TO TAKE THE TIME TO REST and rebuild your strength. Welcome the quiet times that allow you to dispel the false beliefs that have governed your life. The time will come, once again, for taking action toward achieving your goals. Focus on the journey itself rather than on the goal or dream. In this way you will get to experience the joys that abound in each step of the journey. Too often the goal or dream becomes your sole purpose in life.

It is important to enjoy fully the process of achieving your dream. The steps in the process are what bring new growth and understanding, which in turn deepens and expands the dream. The journey that leads to the dream is more important to the growth of the soul than the actual achieving of the goal. The dream has great value for the advancement of the soul, but when the dream becomes more important than the process required to achieve it, the wisdom and integrity of the dream may be lost.

The loftier the dream, the more it influences the lives of others and the greater the need for discernment, wisdom, and integrity along the way. If the dream becomes fueled by self-importance or doubt, it will lose its original purpose and intent. It is better to forego the dream and pursue it at a later date than to dishonor it. A dream from the heart will never utilize acts of dishonor against the self or others for its achievement.

Deem yourself worthy of your dream in its highest form and you will automatically deem others worthy of your respect and integrity. It is your self-worth that is truly the issue. When you feel your true worthiness in every fiber of your being, you will lose the need to condemn others to a state of unworthiness. You will know the joy of your being through letting go of judgment.

Listen to your heart and receive the understanding that you are deserving of your dream. Likewise, you will understand the same about everyone you meet. You will know without doubt that your fellow man is totally deserving of your highest integrity at all times.

As you release the need to judge yourself, the need to judge others will disappear. All action in thought, word, and deed will flow from you through a deserving and worthy heart. You will be able to acknowledge the worthy heart that is present in others. All thoughts of unworthiness will dissolve and be replaced by thoughts of unconditional love for yourself and your fellow man. All are deserving of forgiveness and love. Be a force for worthiness in your own life and set the example for others to follow.

141

Make your journey with a heart filled with wisdom and integrity, and your dreams will expand with higher purpose. Take the journey one step at a time, allowing yourself to receive the joy of being in the present moment. When the path is followed with the joy of experiencing each moment, the dream takes care of itself effortlessly. When each moment is experienced with a deserving heart, the path is lighted and clear.

Live your personal truth in every moment, and greater truth will find its way into your heart. Walk your path with a voice of integrity and wisdom even when others demand much less of you.

Give of yourself from your highest self even when others feel they deserve less. Let them know through your example that you believe they are deserving of all the universe has to offer, and they will feel the warmth of worthiness from within themselves. If they are not ready to receive this warmth, allow their choice and release the need to judge. Know that a seed of worthiness has been planted, and others will come along to help nurture it further.

Always make the journey more important than the goal, and your dreams will be achieved effortlessly. There will never be a need to force attainment of a goal when you trust that God will present opportunities for your growth and the achievement of your purpose. It is only through doubt that this process becomes blocked and obstructed. When doubt surfaces, allow it to teach you of the fears that are still held within.

Enter the silence and enfold yourself in the stillness. In the quiet of meditation, doubt loses its grip. You feel renewed, confident, and worthy. You will open the doorway that allows for new lessons and challenges on your journey. When self-doubt surfaces, allow it to teach you of the false beliefs that hold it in place. Feed your doubt the silence of meditation so that you can dissolve its power and continue on the path with a deserving heart.

Move Forward with
a Confident Heart

⌐ Uriel ⌐

LIVE YOUR LIFE WITH THE JOY that comes from a confident heart. Confidence is what generates the energy to move forward without fear. When your thoughts are focused on judgment of yourself and others, fear is generated rather than confident action. It is difficult to have confidence when judgment is present. The critical mind judges the actions of the past, which leaves you stagnate in the present and fearful of the future. Enter the silence of meditation to still the critical mind and give it the relief from judgment that it seeks.

The cycles of criticism and judgment only serve to strengthen the negative chatter from the mind. In the silence, allow the heart to soothe the mind and free it from the chatter of criticism and judgment. The silence has the power to strengthen the confident heart and still the critical mind.

A confident heart allows you to move forward in life with an acceptance of the self. The heart trusts in the

144

opportunities for growth that exist in the presence of the unknown. The present moment is where the flame of the heart burns. It has no concern for what is past or what the future holds. The heart lives for the joy that is present in this moment.

The mind lives for what it already knows, and it fears the unknown. The mind creates experiences based on what is familiar. If the mind is familiar with pain, sorrow, and suffering, then those are the experiences it will continue to create. These familiar experiences will be projected into the future with concentration on thoughts of the past. The present moment becomes lost and the heart's desires become suppressed with fear.

Peel away the layers of doubt and fear created by the mind by allowing your unconscious mental chatter to become conscious. The layers of self-doubt are exposed and released by the conscious mind. The mind can then embrace positive thoughts that allow for the unknown to be present in your life. In this new, conscious awareness, the present moment can be felt and experienced with a joyous and confident heart.

The heart and mind work together as one to guide the body. The body is then able to respond without fear. Life is a limitless bounty of opportunity for growth. Cherish every moment. Live your life fully and give thanks for the blessings that are present in each day. Allow your confident heart to lead the way and ease your troubled mind. Enter the silence of meditation to create unity between your heart and mind, and move your body forward with confidence.

Embrace Your Shadow

☞ Gabriel ☜

DO NOT FEAR THE SHADOW OR DARKER SIDE OF YOURSELF. There is an abundance of knowledge held by this part of you. Your shadow side holds valuable records and suppressed feelings. In allowing these records to surface, you can learn to express your true feelings in a loving way. As long as you fear your true feelings, you will never allow yourself to express from your heart.

There is nothing in you that is unworthy. Even your hatred and anger are blessings when used to reconnect you with the true feelings within your heart. Allow the darkest parts of yourself to be exposed. Do this without judgment, and you will heal the wounds that hold the dark feelings in place.

Denying the negative thoughts and feelings that you have buried within you gives them the power to control your life. How can you live with joy and self-confidence if your heart is being held hostage by the fear

146

of exposure? Release the negative thoughts and feelings that you have secretly filed away within yourself. Your secret self blocks the way for you to know and embrace your God self. This is your true self.

You live in fear that others will discover your shadow side, and in the discovery, they will deem you unlovable. This is a false belief, and it gives your shadow side the power to control you. When you lack control over yourself, you will have a strong desire to control others. As your shadow side gains strength, the need to control others also strengthens. In order to live from within your heart, the need for control must be released.

Still the mind, and in the quiet, invite the shadow aspects of yourself to teach you. Your inner light will shine brighter because you invited your shadow side to receive the light and love of God that is present within you. Be grateful for the teachings of your shadow side and the opportunity to feel all of who you are more deeply. Be gentle and receive this part of yourself with unconditional love and forgiveness.

There is nothing within you that is unforgivable or unlovable. All that is required is for you to stop hiding from the parts of yourself that generate fear and start forgiving yourself. Allow for God's grace in your life and your life will be filled with grace. When you release your fear and honor the teachings of your shadow side, you are showing yourself the greatest self-love. When you love yourself unconditionally, you are loving God.

Use the power that is present in the silence to slay the dragons of fear and false beliefs that you hold about yourself.

Experience Others with Empathy

≈ *Michael* ≈

THE JOY YOU FEEL WITHIN YOUR HEART is the joy of unifying yourself with God. Unity with God brings a feeling of ecstasy within the body and mind. When you are aligned with God in your heart, it is impossible to think negative thoughts about yourself. You are able to love yourself with true humility. The joyousness you feel has no trace of self-importance or self-doubt. When you are unified with God in your heart, you feel centered and balanced. The need for extremes in your life are dissolved.

This unity creates balance within your experiences. You can now have empathy for the experiences of others in order to gain understanding of their feelings. Through heartfelt unity with God, you can understand them without having to put your body through the physical experience. In this way, you are able to learn the lessons of balance without the physical trauma.

When you experience life through empathy, you use your internal knowing, which is your heartfelt connection with God, to have compassion and understanding for others without having to experience their pain within your body. This is the result of unifying with God in your heart, rather than unifying with other people in order to experience God.

By establishing a unified connection with God in your heart first, you are able to unite with others and form healthy relationships while still maintaining your own individuality. You become balanced within because you are one with God while still maintaining the boundaries of self.

You can achieve this balanced state through meditation and prayer. Then you will be able to unite with other individuals in a healthy way. The need for co-dependency, manipulation, and the controlling of others will disappear from your relationships. You will only form relationships with others who have found unity within their own hearts. Through true humility, you will have compassion and understanding for those souls who are still in the process of opening their inner connection with God.

The joy experienced in this type of human connecting will surpass anything you have ever known. People will be a pleasure to experience because you will no longer be bound to experience them through sympathy. The compassion within your heart will radiate from you to touch the hearts of others. Your own heart will open even wider through the empathic experiences you will share with others.

When you release the sympathetic response of trying to fix the lives of the people you care for, you will be able to enjoy others through an open heart and a loving mind. Strengthen the unity with God from within your heart through the continued practice of prayer and meditation.

About the Author

SINDA JORDAN lives in Colorado with her two daughters. As an intuitive counselor, she helps others develop a personal relationship with the angelic beings that watch over them, guide them, and unconditionally love them. She currently gives workshops based on the teachings of *Inspired by Angels.*